THINK LIKE AN ATHLETE DON'T ACT LIKE ONE

For my MVP's: Wanita, Philippa & Miles

THINK LIKE AN ATHLETE DON'T ACT LIKE ONE

JOOST PLUIJMS

© 2024
Author: Joost Pluijms
Concept: Aernoud Bourdrez and Peter Heykamp
thinklikeapro.org

Production: buro van Ons
Beeld Editor: Frank Schallmaier
Editor: Rodney Bolt
Photo cover: Brian Hill

ISBN 978 90 636 9719 8
1st printing 2024

The author is member of 1% for the Planet.

BIS Publishers
Borneostraat 80-A
1094 CP Amsterdam
T +31 (0)20 515 02 30
bis@bispublishers.com
bispublishers.com

WHAT YOU DIDN'T KNOW ABOUT ATHLETES

Elite sports are hard (work). Blood, sweat, and tears on the track, mat, or field. But, in reality, we actually see very little of the actual real battleground. The true battle takes place between the ears.

As a sports psychologist and scientist, I've had the privilege of working with exceptional athletes, coaches, and teams for years. From sailing to BMX Freestyle, and from hockey to alpine skiing. What makes them belong to the elite? Their mental game. This book unlocks the mental secrets of sports legends from around the world. Not just for athletes, but for anyone who wants to lead their daily life like a champion.

In this book, you'll find 75 lessons you won't encounter in a standard sports book. You'll learn the importance of a 'nappuccino,' how to see like a champion, why you should do a 'Tony Hawk', and how Epke Zonderland wins even before he touches the horizontal bar. This book is your personal playbook.

Prepare for the challenges, peak at the right moment, and recover stronger than ever. Make the most of what you have, but do it your way. And don't forget: sports are fun.

Joost Pluijms

"A must-read to train your resilience!"
Nienke Nijenhuis, Director of Sports, BrabantSport, home of TeamNL

CONTENT

Pssst... read more?

Dive into the core of sports psychology with these essential works: **Frank Bakker** and **Raôul Oudejans** reveal powerful skills and strategies in **"Sportpsychologie"**, while **Gijs Jansen** teaches us about psychological flexibility in **"ACT in groepen"** and **"How 2 ACT"**. **Afke van de Wouw** offers dual insights with **"Leren Presteren"** and **"Leren Revalideren"** (co-authored with **Yara Van Gendt**), crucial for any athlete aiming for peak performance and effective recovery. **Marjolein Torenbeek's "Synergie"** explores the dynamics of teamwork, and **Nico van Yperen**, with his deep dive into mental resilience in **"Focus, Vertrouwen, en Veerkracht"**, enhances the mental toolkit of every athlete. Finally, **René Wormhoudt**, **Jan Willem Teunissen**, and **Geert Savelsbergh** bring a revolutionary approach to talent development with the **"Athletic Skills Model"**. **More tips?** Email: **joost@pluijms.com**

START WITH YOUR FAREWELL

An original, signed Michael 'Air Jump' Jordan offered at an auction.

Michael Jordan, the undisputed master of basketball, had one clear goal from the start of his career: to be remembered as the greatest. Jordan understood like no other that it is not just about winning as many games as possible, but more importantly: what will you leave behind that is truly worthwhile for future generations.

During my time as a sports psychologist at NAC Breda, I always asked footballers: "What will your farewell speech sound like?" In other words: how do you want the world to remember you? What values are important to you? These questions are far from simple, but they provide indispensable clarity and direction to your ambitions. Let legends like Jordan inspire you: transform into the athlete you wish to be, driven by your values.

And write that speech. ■

THE TRUE POWER OF A TEAM

The most successful basketball team of the '90s: Chicago Bulls.

True strength lies not in the talent of an individual but in unity and shared goals. According to team psychologist Marjolein Torenbeek, the true magic of a team is the synergy, where individuals merge into an invincible unity. The Chicago Bulls, with legends like Jordan, Pippen, and Rodman, illustrate this perfectly. Despite their differing personalities, their success was the sum of mutual respect, clear role distribution, mutual trust, and one common goal. ■

GIVE THAT VOICE A NAME

Mascot Harry of the Atlanta Hawks basketball team in Georgia, USA.

Will readers even buy this book? Everyone knows that little voice in their head telling them what they're doing isn't good enough. Or what if you fail? That sometimes-wise voice pops up at the most unexpected moments and meddles in everything. Whether you want it to or not.

Psychologist Gijs Jansen had found an effective remedy for this. He gives his critical voice a pet name and thanks it every now and then for its input. Afterward, he can fully focus on the things that really matter again. The better you learn to observe them from a distance, the less they will affect you. You are not your thoughts.

By the way, my inner voice is named James, a rebellious butler.

THE DILEMMA OF A SPORTS PARENT

Richard Williams with his daughter Venus during a training session, 1990.

As a parent in competitive sports, you walk a fine line. Your role is not just to encourage your child but also to nurture a love for the sport. Why does your child play? That drive should be cherished, regardless of wins or losses, engagement or withdrawal. The stories of the Krajiceks, the Williams sisters, and Agassi reveal the raw side of this world, where parental support can sometimes turn into unhealthy pressure. But these stories also offer a powerful lesson: sports parenting is about fostering joy and creating an environment where children can thrive not just as athletes, but as individuals. At the heart of it all lies unconditional love - the strongest motivation there is. ∎

TAKE A NAPPUCCINO

Lionel Messi, a day after winning the 2023 World Cup final.

Topsport Topics frequently publishes factsheets with useful scientific information for sports practice. For instance, caffeine increases alertness, reaction time, and vigilance. Endurance athletes who consume 3 to 6 milligrams of caffeine per kilogram of body weight (3 to 6 cups of coffee) can expect an improvement of around 3 percent in exertions lasting more than 30 minutes.

Sleep also affects performance: short afternoon naps of up to 30 minutes can give athletes a significant boost. Caffeine and sleep turn out to be a golden combination. My recipe: grab a cappuccino, take a power nap of no more than 30 minutes, and when you wake up, they both kick in and you perform optimally.

Forget doping, take a nappuccino. ■

NERVES
ARE
NORMAL

Tom Dumoulin was in the lead during the 2017 Giro d'Italia but had to stop for a poop moment.

What if your legs begin to hurt while cycling? Don't panic. It's part of the process. Fellow sports psychologist Kelly Dekker once put it beautifully: confidence comes after you start, not before. Think of Tom Dumoulin who, during a critical moment in the Giro d'Italia, had to stop for a 'poop moment'. He didn't let it distract him and still won the stage. You can overcome even the greatest challenges, nerves and all. ■

WRITE IT OFF

A disappointed fan after the lost match against Costa Rica during the World Cup in Qatar.

Fact: Every day, we have an average of 40,000 till 60,000 thoughts, and most of them are nonsense. That is why, as a sports psychologist, I frequently use the 3R model with athletes: Register, Release, and Refocus. Let's start with the first R, conceived by the Danish sports psychologists Henriksen, Hansen, and Hvid Larsen.

It often helps to regularly register your thoughts and feelings before or after a game; positive, negative, whatever they may be. Writing them down means not using your head as a storage space. What's more, writing allows you to distance yourself from your thoughts, so they cannot deceive you.

Want to know what the second and third Rs are? Then keep reading. ■

SMELL THE GRASS!

Semifinal of the Olympic Games in Japan between Japan and Spain, 2021.

I once coached a talented soccer goalkeeper who was easily distracted and, as a result, got frustrated. Together, we worked on the second R of the 3R model: release. As soon as he noticed he was distracted, I asked him to shift his attention to something he could see, hear, feel, and smell. The exercise lasted only about 20-30 seconds. He would then look at the left corner of the opposite goal, the penalty spot, and smell the freshly cut grass. This helped him to shift his focus from inside his head to the outside world. Then, he would recall his priorities and the actions needed to meet them. This way, he was ready for the next ball, for the next save. ∎

YOU DON'T HAVE TO BE SUPERMAN

Headcoach Mourinho during the 2010 UEFA Champions League final.

Even the greatest strategists in sports experience moments of doubt and uncertainty. Take José Mourinho, a master of mental warfare. The UEFA Champions League final between Bayern Munich and his Inter Milan in 2010 was just such a moment for him. But Mourinho didn't panic. On the contrary, he used the pressure to refocus his team. How? He created an 'us against the world' mentality by highlighting his players' strengths. This moment of reflection, of finding calm under pressure, and the art of the 3rd R - Refocus - sets great athletes and teams apart from the rest. And it shows that you don't have to be Superman to win, as long as you master the 3Rs: Register, Release, Refocus. ■

BE
KIND
TO
YOURSELF

Johnny Hoogerland after falling into barbed wire during the Tour de France, 2011.

In the world of sports, athletes are unrelenting towards themselves, especially in the face of setbacks. Take the case of cyclist Johnny Hoogerland who, during the Tour de France, crashed into barbed wire. Despite the intense pain and injuries, he pedaled on.

Imagine if your best friend went through this. You would undoubtedly advise them to ease up, to be kind to themselves. Why not extend the same grace to yourself? Self-compassion is not a sign of weakness; it is a testament to mental strength. Let Hoogerland inspire you to resilience, but remember: be your own best friend. ■

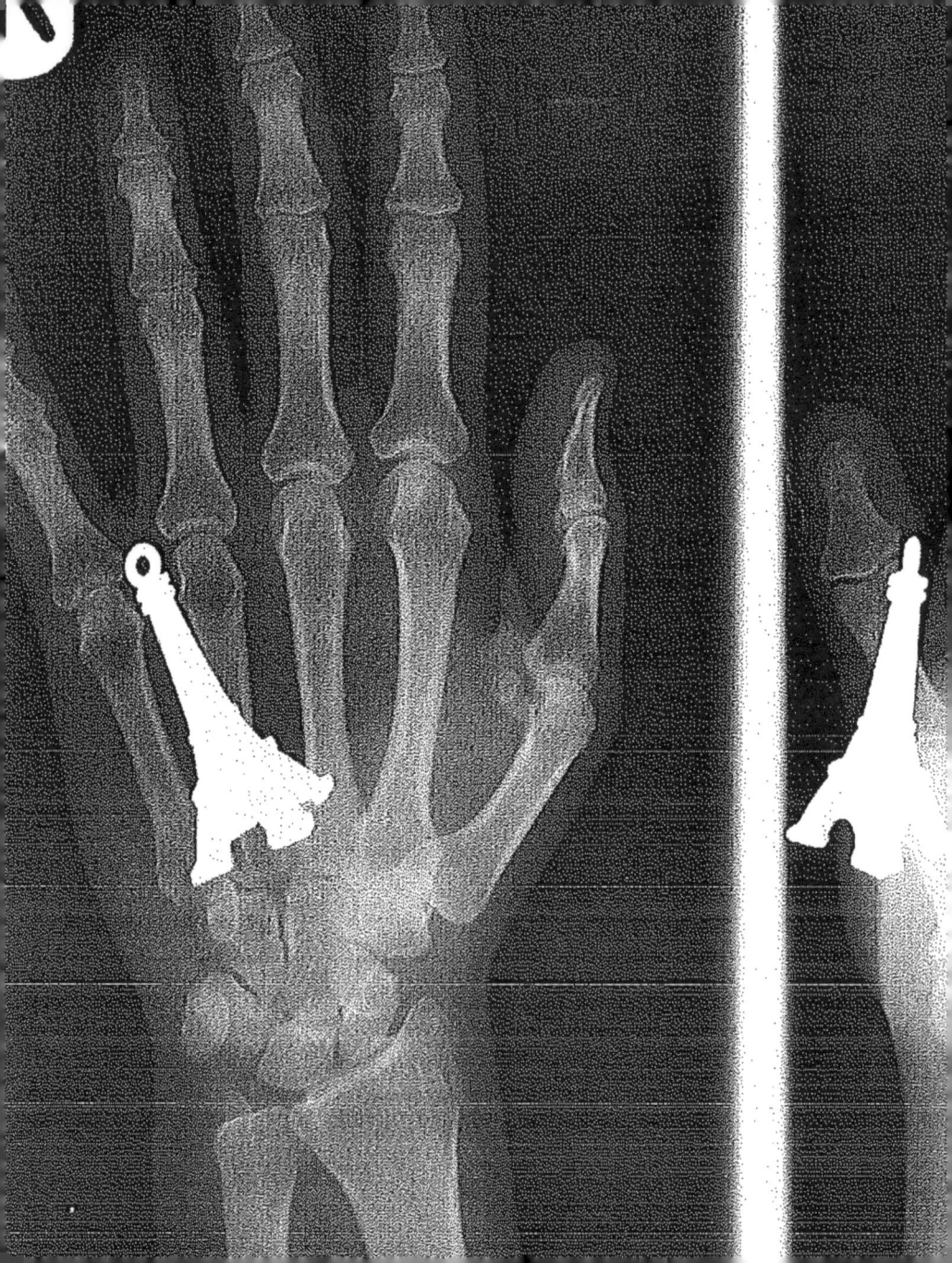

RECOVERY IN PRIME FORM

An X-ray of a jogger who fell and had a souvenir keyring pierced her hand.

Injuries are what athletes perhaps fear the most. Not illogically, as they flirt with the boundary between intense training and overtraining. Previously, sports psychology was mainly employed for performance enhancement. Nowadays, it is also used for preventing injuries and for recovery post-injury. The book "Leren Revalideren", by sports psychologists Afke van de Wouw and Yara van Gendt, is entirely focused on this aspect. They discuss which mental factors can influence injury (such as stress), how to process your injury, and what tools you can use during your rehabilitation, even when facing setbacks. Think about setting realistic goals, visualization, enhancing your resilience, and systematically applying breathing and relaxation exercises. So, you don't have to be sidelined during your rehabilitation. Many athletes even say they come out stronger. It almost makes you want to have an injury. ■

MAY THE FLOW BE WITH YOU

Norwegian athlete Asbjorg Nesje trains in front of The Opera House in Oslo for the 2023 Death Diving World Championship (Døds).

Flow, that magical moment when everything clicks into place and your performance effortlessly propels you to the top. Every athlete dreams of it. Capturing that state of being feels like a sport in itself. Flow doesn't appear on command and, fortunately, isn't necessary for great achievements or pure enjoyment. Yet, experiencing it is an unparalleled pleasure. Increase your chances of flow by ensuring a perfect alignment between skills and challenges, with crystal clear goals and undivided focus. Then, you find yourself in a realm of complete control, so effortless that time loses its grip. May the flow be with you. ■

#13

EMOTIONS ARE EFFECTIVE

A young Everton supporter cheers on his team against Stevenage.

Emotions are often seen as a burden. However, psychologist Susan David argues the opposite is true. Emotions provide crucial data for every individual. A broader emotional vocabulary improves your ability to discern and regulate feelings, even in interactions with others, like your coach. Vincent Siderius and Sebastian Buurma's emotion meter can often offer athletes insight: is your energy high or low, is a feeling pleasant or unpleasant? This distinction helps them to recognize, understand, and appropriately label emotions. Regular check-ins with the emotion meter help. Anger, frustration, and irritation; joy, optimism, or a festive mood - each points to something different. The better you understand them, the better you can respond. ∎

FOUR CAPTAINS ON ONE SHIP

Head coach Israel Gonzalez during a European basketball game between Partizan Belgrade and Alba.

Increasingly, I see coaches employing multiple leaders within a team. They understand that motivation and performance can be improved with shared leadership. Professor Katrien Fransen defines four informal leadership roles: task and motivational leaders on the field; social and external leaders off the field. Each role is essential for the functioning of a sports team. I often let team members choose the informal leaders themselves. Every time, I am surprised by the positive result: fewer conflicts and more motivation.

#15

EMBRACE YOUR COMPETITOR

Dorian van Rijsselberghe (right) and Kiran Badloe win gold and silver respectively at the 2018 Sailing World Championships in Aarhus, Denmark.

After their friendly Olympic rivalry for a single Tokyo ticket, windsurfers Kiran Badloe and Dorian van Rijsselberghe embraced each other. It was one of the most beautiful hugs I have ever seen. The pupil, Badloe, defeated the master, Van Rijsselberghe, a two-time gold medalist. For years, the two men sought each other out daily to improve their skills; together, they were the world's absolute best. Don't avoid your competitor; move towards them. That way, you can reach the top together. ■

#16

PERFORM UNDER PRESSURE

French surfer Eric Rebiere during The Nazaré Tow Surfing Challenge competition in Portugal.

Optimizing skills, minimizing errors. That's where we as sports psychologists come in. Mistakes usually happen under pressure. By practicing under pressure, you ultimately make fewer mistakes. Football coach Foppe de Haan once devised a drill for Ruud van Nistelrooy during his time at SC Heerenveen: he allowed Van Nistelrooy to take only one penalty after training, no more. If he missed, there was no second chance to score. Don't be alarmed: your performance may temporarily decline, but with repeated exposure, your performance will actually improve. So, it is not necessarily about practicing more, but about how you practice. ■

TRUST YOUR OWN WAY

Scooby Doo (with dog) gets ready to participate in the UK Dog Surfing Championships in Bournemouth, England.

Every athletic body is built differently. There isn't one optimal way of moving or approach. In my career, I have coached two top sailors with completely different tactics and styles of sailing. Yet, they each sailed just as fast. There is no right way, only the right way for you. ■

18

FROM TRIP-UP TO TROPHY

Boston Marathon 1967 - Race official Jock Semple attempts to physically push Kathrine Switzer out of the race, as she (illegally) becomes the first woman to run in the event.

Success is not a straight line but a path filled with bumps, detours, and yes, even setbacks. Every time you fall, you plant the seeds for your next victory. Take Kathrine Switzer, the first woman to complete the Boston Marathon, even as people tried physically to stop her. Her struggle and perseverance have not only shaped her own career, but also paved the way for female athletes around the world. Embrace setbacks, just like Switzer. Analyze what happened, adjust your strategy, and come back stronger. It is the art of reflection that ultimately makes you invincible. Stumble? Struggle. Shine! ■

19

MASTER THE CHAOS

Michael Phelps swims to gold at the 2008 Olympic Games in Beijing, China.

Most athletes like to have control over their thoughts and feelings. Unfortunately, that is an illusion. You cannot change the waves in the sea, but you can learn how to surf them. During the 200 meter butterfly in Beijing, Michael Phelps' goggles filled with water. For most swimmers, this would be a disaster, but Phelps remained calm. He had counted his strokes and the length of the pool so often during training that he knew exactly where he was, even though he couldn't see anything. He went on to break the world record. ■

20

THE
WHAT
IF
SCENARIO

Old lady with a walker crosses the road during a professional cycling race in Etten-Leur, the Netherlands.

Mathieu van der Poel grew up in a cycling family, but that's not necessarily what sets him apart from others. His approach does. He is the embodiment of scenario planning in sports. Before every race, he carefully studies his rivals and outlines multiple scenarios. With a mix of precision and elements of surprise, he thus steers the race in his favor, always one step ahead. And as a spectator, you know that when Mathieu van der Poel is competing, you're in for a surprise.

21

DOLCE FAR NIENTE

The Dutch football team Feyenoord cools down in a stream in Austria after a training session.

Sports psychologist Yannick Balk completed his PhD. on the mental recovery process of elite athletes. He explored the impact of insufficient recovery, and unveiled effective strategies for recovery and performance enhancement. His conclusion: the ability to occasionally detach yourself from sports or work is crucial. So, consciously reserve time for yourself. Allow yourself a day where you have the freedom to choose what you do - or don't do - and with whom. After all, mental relaxation is deeply personal. I emphasized the importance of Balk's advice in a workshop for doctors and nurses during the challenging COVID-19 pandemic. Especially in times of high pressure, it is essential to embrace the art of "Dolce far niente", or the sweetness of doing nothing. It not only provides a much-needed break for your mind but also enhances your ability to perform when it really matters. ∎

22

IT TAKES LONGER THAN YOU THINK

A record injury time during a football match in Israel.

American cognitive scientist Douglas Hofstadter has come up with a law stating: "It always takes longer than you expect, even when you take into account Hofstadter's Law."

People tend to underestimate the time it takes to complete a task. Top athletes are no exception. Take the soccer match which ran to a record 42 minutes of injury time. Be flexible in your planning and allow room for the unexpected. Hofstadter's law serves not only as a reminder of our limitations when it comes to estimating time, but also as a call for exercise discretion and preparation for life's unpredictability. ■

23

SOMETIMES NOT

Dressed as Smurfs in France during an attempt to set a record for the largest gathering of Smurfs.

Every athlete has their own vision of who they are. However, being too attached to a rigid self-image can really be a hindrance. So, how do you give yourself some space? Psychologist Steven Hayes has a clever method for doing this. He first asks a client to describe themselves with "I am...", followed by two positive descriptions and one negative. Like "I am cheerful. I am enthusiastic. I am a poor loser."

Then comes the twist: each statement is followed by a comma and "and sometimes not." The athlete repeats the crafted sentences and lets the realization sink in. "I am cheerful, and sometimes not. I am enthusiastic, and sometimes not. I am a poor loser, and sometimes not."

This exercise provides relief. After all, no one is constantly the same, and that's a good thing. ■

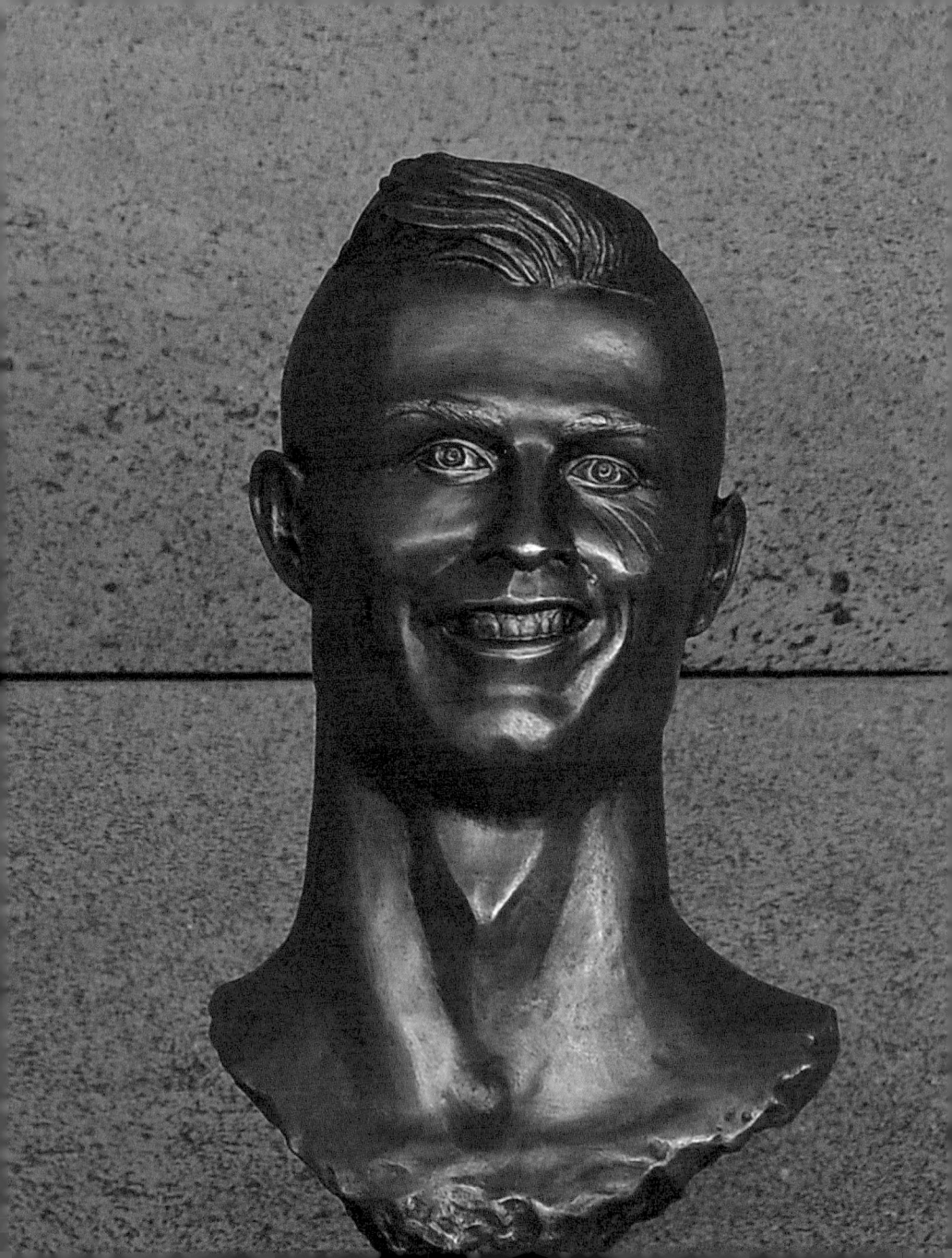

SEE LIKE
A CHAMPION

A bust of footballer Cristiano Ronaldo at Madeira Airport, Portugal.

Imagine this: I see exactly what Lionel Messi sees, but delivering the perfect pass at the crucial moment? That's beyond me. The connection between perception and action is what distinguishes true champions from the rest. Cristiano Ronaldo has demonstrated how he can score, even if the lights go out before the ball reaches him. Together with Niek Pot, we investigated this phenomenon among top hockey goalkeepers during a penalty corner. We positioned a screen so that goalkeepers could see only crucial moments. This revealed that elite athletes focus on essential information leading to the right decisions and actions. Sometimes, it is even better to ignore certain information and concentrate on what truly matters. ■

#25

PAY ATTENTION TO THE OUTCOME OF YOUR MOVEMENT

British Free-climber Adam Lockwood during a stunt in Barcelona, Spain.

Sports psychologist and movement scientist Raôul Oudejans had basketball players practice with a special pair of glasses. These glasses limited the view of the basket until the critical moment just before the shot. This forced the players to use the goal of their action - the basket - as their external focal point, rather than the execution of their shot. It demonstrates how crucial it is to direct your concentration on what you aim to achieve rather than on the execution itself. It trains us to trust our skills and intuition, focused on the result, even when the path there is uncertain. Focus on the end result of your actions; the movements you need to make will follow naturally. ■

26

CREATE YOUR PATH

Slovenian Janja Garnbret creates her own path during the qualifiers at the the world climbing championships in Innsbruck, Austria.

In 2019, Slovenian climber Janja Garnbret astounded the world by becoming the first athlete ever to win all six World Cup bouldering events in a single season. This unprecedented achievement not only showcases her dominance in the sport but also her ability to find a successful, often innovative approach for each climb. Garnbret is renowned for her ability to 'read' routes and opt for moves that others either shy away from or overlook. This approach enables her to solve complex problems in unique ways, thereby creating her own path. ■

27

LIFE
AFTER
DEATH

In 1974, Frenchman Philippe Petit walked between the then-extant Twin Towers in New York, at a height of 400 meters without any safety gear.

It is often said that an athlete dies twice: once as an athlete and once as a person. If you have given your all to your sport, who are you when that comes to an end? Perhaps the greatest loss is the identity you derive from your sport. What many athletes don't realize is that they often acquire numerous skills during their careers that are useful after their time at the top of their sport ends. Sports Psychology professor Nico van Yperen identifies the following skills: goal setting, disciplined work, and performing under pressure. A well-prepared athlete doesn't retire; they just switch careers. That is why I advise athletes to start thinking about this during their sports heyday. ■

28

YOU HAVE ONE CHANCE

Use the white circle as your target.

The first can be your last. That motto helps me. Sometimes, I speak with athletes or coaches only once, for example, during a consultation hour. This challenges me to work efficiently and effectively. Even one session can be valuable. By using brief interventions, you can create radical change. This way of working, known as single-session therapy, is becoming increasingly popular within psychology. The premise is that people only want and need one session. How does it work? Focus on one important point, not broadly, but deeply. Then, leverage the strengths and skills the individual already possesses and engage their environment for support. Minor course corrections at the right moment can have a significant impact in the long run.

29

TRAIN IN YOUR MIND

Dutch gymnast Epke Zonderland's golden dismount at the 2012 London Olympics.

Visualization is the key to ultimate mastery. Olympic gymnastics champion Epke Zonderland first practiced all his horizontal bar routines in his mind before starting the competition. It's an effective method that requires minimal effort, but yields maximum results. It activates the same areas of the brain and muscles as the actual physical performance.

In a Nike commercial, you see how soccer legend Lewandowski sits on a sofa the night before a game, and visualizes himself dribbling the ball across the field, dodging a tackle, and ultimately scoring. Visualization is your invisible training partner, leading you to success, time and again. You can continue training this way, even with an injury. ■

30

SPY WITH STYLE

Finn Bilous from New Zealand performs a freestyle run during the 2022 Olympic Games in Beijing, China.

Watching is just as important as doing. Athletes know this better than anyone. They refine their skills by analyzing the movements and methods of their rivals before and during performances without taking any risks themselves. This art of observation turns every fellow athlete into an unsolicited guide. Let the world be your teacher. Pay attention to successful tactics both within and outside your field. Observe how problems are solved in other contexts and consider whether you can adapt these solutions to your own situations. Whether it's an innovative presentation technique, a fresh approach to customer service, or a creative fix for a routine task, there are lessons everywhere. Step into the shoes of a 'spy with style': observe, absorb, and implement. ■

#31

FRILUFTSLIV

A player scores a try during the Water Rugby event organized by the Lausanne University Club in Lausanne, Switzerland.

Do you feel the urge to venture into nature? That call is more than just a desire; it's a recipe for well-being. In Scandinavia, they call it 'Friluftsliv' - living in the open air. And yes, backed up by scientific research: nature heals. Around the world, doctors are increasingly prescribing 'nature therapy' to harmonize body and mind. The result? Relaxation, joy, and a calm mind. As a sports psychologist, I experience it myself: nature stimulates my creativity and strengthens my connection with clients. Leave the consulting room, nature is calling! ■

32

GOLDEN HABIT

Rafael Nadal requests his towel from a ball boy during his quarterfinal match at Roland-Garros in 2018.

An athlete I coached once confessed to me that he always put on his left sock first. Was that normal? I asked him if he was familiar with the 19 routines of tennis player Rafael Nadal: entering the court with a racket in his hand, always stepping over a line with his right foot, jumping during the coin toss, and using his towel after every point. A fixed sequence of actions can serve as a trigger to enter the right mental state. The routine increases concentration and leaves less room for distraction. It provides a sense of security, as long as there is some degree of flexibility. Note: routines are especially effective in sports where you can determine the pace - at least to some extent. Like tennis. ∎

33

THE YOGURT CHALLENGE

The author of this book Joost Pluijms, takes a yogurt shower himself, in accordance with Acceptance and Commitment Therapy.

Sounds crazy? That's exactly the point. The yogurt challenge is a hilarious yet profound exercise from Acceptance and Commitment Therapy. It playfully introduces you to accepting unusual situations and feelings. A yogurt shower immerses you in all kinds of thoughts, but it also teaches you that it is okay to do things outside your comfort zone. What's more, the cold, odd sensation of yogurt on your skin is not just a physical experience; it symbolizes breaking through the barriers of conventional thinking patterns. Sometimes, you need to immerse yourself in the unknown to truly be free in your thoughts and actions. Are you up for it?

34

A BLESSING IN DISGUISE

Australian Steven Bradbury wins short track gold in the 1,000 meters at Salt Lake City, thanks to all his competitors falling.

Luck plays a significant lead role in the script of success. Australian short-track speed skater Steven Bradbury won a gold medal against all odds when all his competitors crashed just before the finish line. Pure luck. Many athletes and coaches tend to view luck as a marginal factor, something outside their control. As a sports psychologist, I stress: talent and hard work are crucial, but never underestimate the power of a fortunate set of circumstances. It's precisely this unpredictability that makes sports - and life - so fascinating. Sometimes, all you need for a breakthrough is a bit of luck at the right moment. ■

35

SWEEP WITH FEELING

Plastic rats from the Florida Panthers are swept off the ice following the National Hockey League final at the Miami Arena, USA.

Curling teaches us that every little movement counts. Careful sweeping of the ice ensures that you can steer the course of the stone perfectly. A subtle movement of the hand has a huge effect. And this isn't limited to this winter sport alone. It's often those small actions, minute adjustments, or the invisible pat on the back that hold the greatest power. Whether you're preparing a presentation, encouraging a friend, or eating healthily every day, sweeping your way through each day with feeling and precision brings your dreams and goals within reach. ■

36

IMPERFECTLY VALUABLE

A soccer field in São Paulo, Brazil.

Are you striving for a perfect game? Then you are often chasing an elusive deal. This pursuit can lead to stress, loneliness, and a limited view of life. I have coached a top athlete who scored high on Mark Schuls' Sport Perfectionism Test. The pressure of perfectionism held her back. By experimenting with small, error-prone tasks, she learned the value of imperfection and the importance of daring to fail. It's like cooking spaghetti for the first time. She discovered that she was more than her achievements, that making mistakes is part of growth, and that she mattered as a person. Through a task-oriented approach and positive self-reflection, she was able to partly shed the yoke of perfectionism. ∎

37

USE THE AUDIENCE

Football supporters of CSKA during the Champions League match against Tottenham Hotspur in Moscow, Russia.

An audience provides power. Research as early as the 20th century showed that cyclists rode faster when spectators lined the track, a phenomenon known as social facilitation. Spectators can boost your energy level, make you more alert and driven. If you are skilled at your task, then an audience acts as a turbocharger. Covid-19 brought empty stadiums and an echoing silence where cheers once rang out. Athletes accustomed to the energy of the crowd had to tap into a different source. This period highlighted the importance of inner strength and the unique connection between athlete and spectator. It taught us that we can achieve a great performance even in silence, but with the roar of the crowd, we achieve the unthinkable. ∎

38

CULTIVATE YOUR SUCCESS

Two players from Rood Wit '58 celebrate their goal in Voorthuizen, Netherlands.

Stars cannot shine everywhere, meaning performance is often bound to context. That's the conclusion of research by Harvard professor Boris Groysberg on the mobility of top performers. Groysberg advocates developing talent within your own organization. A practical example is AZ Alkmaar's youth academy, which excels in cultivating its own stars. Are you opting for a top athlete from outside? Then be patient. You need to build true growth and success in tandem with each other. Focus on the long term and ensure a strong, supportive environment. That's how you cultivate success. ∎

39

EMBRACE A COMPLIMENT

Diego Maradona (right) embraces Lionel Messi after the quarterfinal against Germany during the 2010 World Cup in Cape Town.

The moment I challenged a volleyball team to give each other compliments on the spot, everything changed. The rule was simple: say thank you when someone compliments you and then keep quiet. Initially, they were skeptical, but once they got the hang of it and learned to cherish a compliment, we saw pride and satisfaction skyrocket. Emotions are contagious, let them work in your favor. One tip: observe carefully before you say something nice. Consider it an ode to esteem. ∎

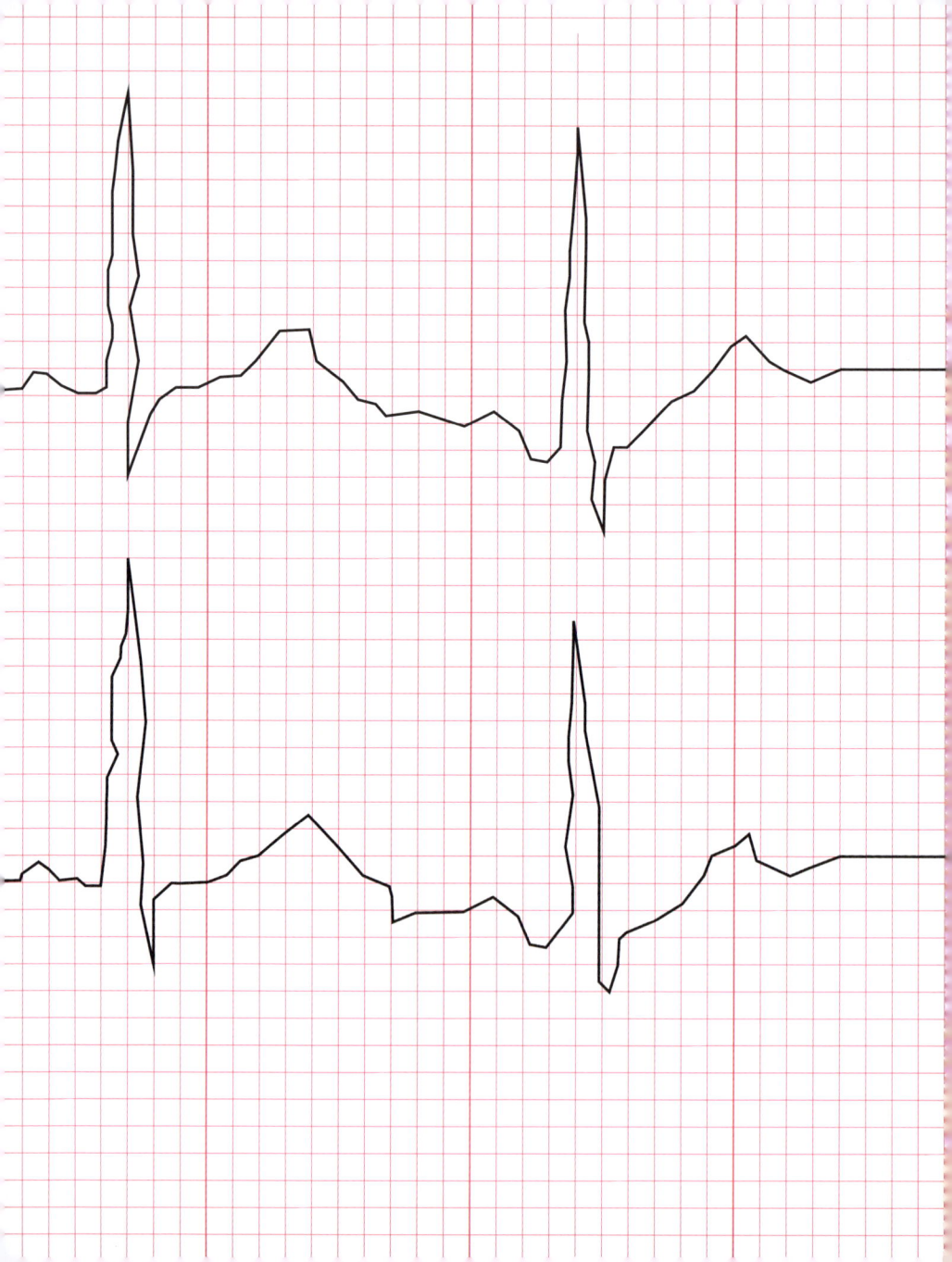

#40

LISTEN TO YOUR HEART

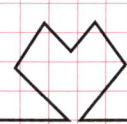

Heart Rate Variability (HRV) is like being sensitive to your body's fine-tuning; it tells you when you're at your best or when you need to ease off. Technology like Kana Daily Life, a biofeedback sensor, helps you track your HRV. This gives you a personal stress manager at your fingertips. High HRV? You're ready to go full throttle. Low HRV? Time for rest and recovery. Athletes have long understood this; they tailor their training based on their personal HRV range for optimal performance and recovery. But everyone can derive benefit from this. Listen more to your heart: it whispers the secrets of stress and recovery. ■

41

ENERGY ALWAYS WINS

Sprinter Usain Bolt's spikes and a sweat print are left on the running track after a training session in Kingston, Jamaica.

Usain Bolt ran a world record 100 meters in 9.58 seconds. His formula for success: don't train too much, recharge your energy in good time. Choosing what energizes you is also my secret weapon. With a vulnerability to bipolar disorder, my life is a constant dance of accelerating and braking. Too little energy? Step on the gas. Too much? Ease off. This balancing act has taught me something crucial: success is largely dependent on how you manage and divide up your energy. I assign a score to every activity for the energy it gives me. This way, I consciously choose the things that steer me towards more well-being, happiness, and success. Your game, your rules. ■

#42

KNOW /
EAT WHAT
YOU DO

British cyclist Mark Cavendish receives bananas after winning a stage of the Tour of Turkey, 2015.

In sports, the line between peak fitness and imbalance is razor-thin. For many athletes, nutrition is both a source of strength and an Achilles' heel. Sports psychologist Karin de Bruin, founder of (W)EET WAT JE DOET [a Dutch pun meaning 'Know / Eat What You Do'], focuses on preventing eating issues in sports and dance. Through workshops, training sessions, and inspiration sessions for athletes, coaches, parents, and boards, they aim to promote healthy performance. The earlier eating behavior disorders are recognized and treated, the better. Factors that help prevent them include a positive attitude towards nutrition and appearance, minimal emphasis on weight, good examples of nutrition and eating behavior, and a healthy relationship among athletes. Make nutrition your ally, not your enemy. ∎

43

FIGHT WITH FIRE

Dutch athlete Sifan Hassan celebrates her victory at the finish line of her first-ever marathon, London, 2023.

In the chaos of the London Marathon, Sifan Hassan proved that success comes not just from the strength of your legs but from the fire in your heart. Her debut was more than just a race; it was a battle against expectations, against the chaos of falls, and against her own limits. Sifan showed that true champions are made by facing challenges with character and courage. Sometimes the path is unpredictable, filled with obstacles you didn't see coming. But remember: it is your response to these moments that defines you. Use your energy wisely, save your strength for when it's truly needed, and let your character lead you to the finish line. Just like Sifan. ■

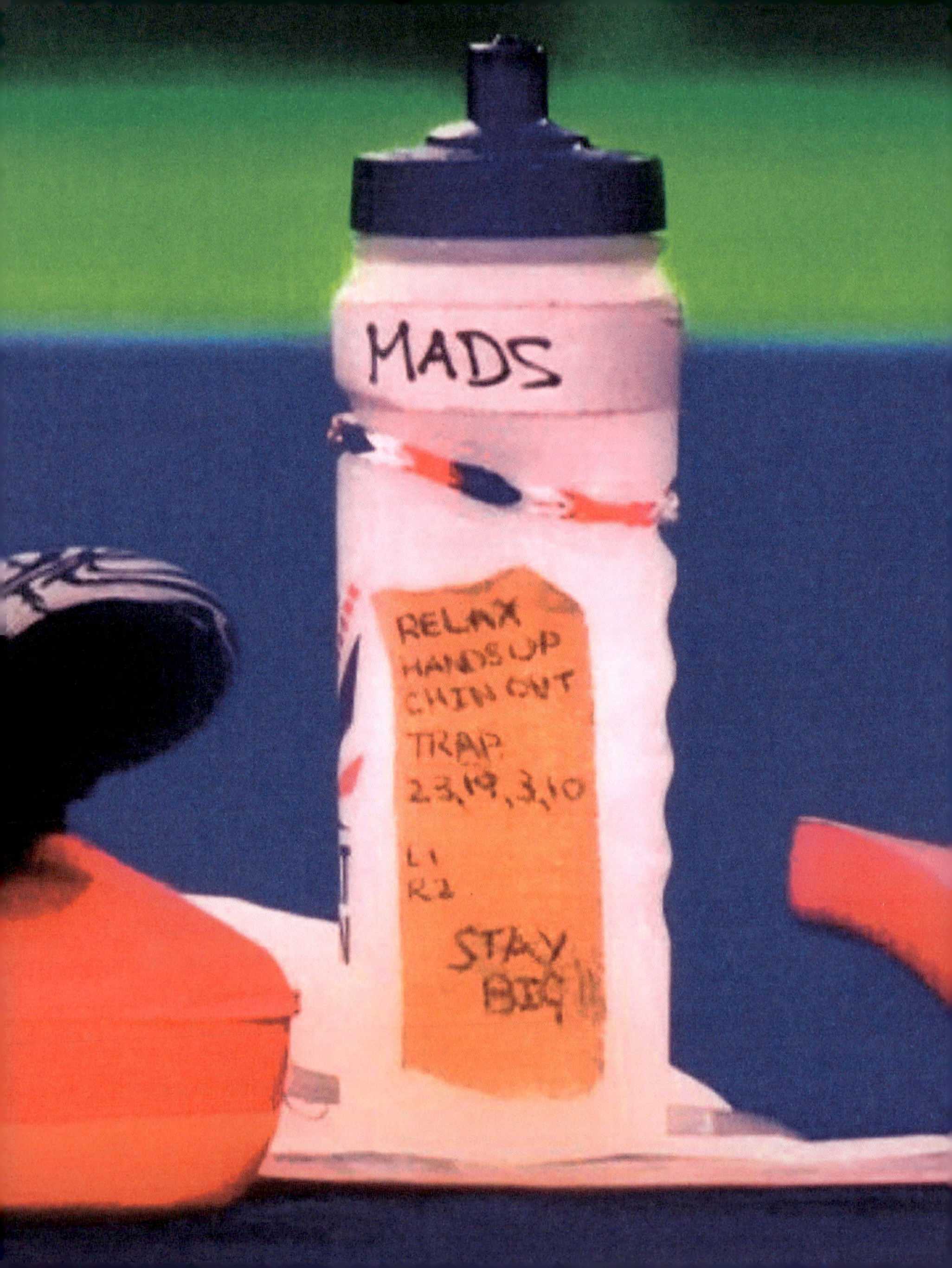
MADS
RELAX
HANDS UP
CHIN OUT
TRAP
23,19,3,10
L1
R2
STAY BIG

44

FIND A WATER BOTTLE

The water bottle of goalkeeper Maddie Hinch after the Olympic hockey final victory against the Netherlands, Rio de Janeiro, Brazil, 2016.

During the tense final of the 2016 Olympics, hockey goalkeeper Maddie Hinch had a water bottle with all sorts of reminders pasted on the side. 'Relax', 'Hands Up', 'Chill Out', 'Stay Big' - they served as anchor points in the heat of battle. This simple but effective technique helped her clinch the victory. Never underestimate the undeniable value of visual reminders. Translate your goals, qualities, or strategies into visual cues. Such a 'water bottle' can help remind you of what's truly important, especially at moments when you need it most. ∎

45

KEEP, STOP, START

The Rugby players of New Zealand perform the Haka in South Africa.

This simple yet revolutionary method provides a powerful framework for team development, inspired by the unmatched team spirit of the All Blacks. It consists of three steps:

Keep: Anchor what brings success.
Stop: Say goodbye to what doesn't work.
Start: Adopt new strategies.

'Keep, stop, start' is the key to a champion team: critical self-examination and collective growth lead to improvement. From sports teams to the corporate world. Embrace this method and transform your team into a world-class unit. ∎

46

SMILE!

A party mask of tennis player Roger Federer.

If there's anyone who smiles a lot, it's Roger Federer, a master on the tennis court. And while it certainly reflects his love for the game, his composure also acts as a psychological disruptor. His ability to remain positive even under intense pressure demoralizes opponents and showcases the power of mental resilience. This tactic underlines that your mental attitude is just as crucial as your physical skill. Don't let setbacks discourage you. A positive demeanor, like a smile, can not only boost your own morale but also influence the dynamics of competition. Use it as both a shield and a sword. ■

47

USE
A BUFFER

Panama striker Luis Tejada argues with the referee.

In the past, referees had only the red card in their back pocket, the yellow was in their shirt. Players immediately knew bad news was coming if a referee reached for his backside. Nowadays, both cards are kept in the chest pocket, usually in a black book. If a referee is not yet sure about the color, he can first just take out the book. He allows himself a short moment of reflection, waits for the players' reactions, listens to comments from assistants through his earpiece, and then decides on yellow or red. Make sure you can always buy time in tricky situations. ■

48

JOY IS ESSENTIAL

Dutch F1 driver Max Verstappen and teammate Sergio Perez from Mexico during the Grand Prix of Monaco.

One of the first things I ask athletes is: when was the last time you truly had fun? The world of competitive sports is tough. Willpower, determination, perseverance - these are only useful if the foundation is joy. Joy is a necessary ingredient, as sports psychologist Tim Koning beautifully outlines in his book on talent. So: when was the last time you experienced joy? What were you doing then? Can you do that again now? ∎

49

ALLIGATOR ON THE GREEN?

A nearly 4-meter-long alligator on the green at Myakka Pines Golf Club, in Englewood, Florida, USA.

Psychologist Daniel Wegner's paradox reveals that the more we focus on what we do NOT want—such as a ball in the water hazard—the greater the chance that is exactly what happens. How ironic. Standing on the golf course with a challenging water hazard ahead? Don't say, "I must not hit the water." Instead, imagine your ball elegantly bypassing the obstacle and safely landing on the fairway. This mental game shifts your focus from avoidance to achievement. ∎

#50

CELEBRATE EVERY INCH

American golfer Patrick Reed celebrates his 2023 victory with a 'Shoey' in Adelaide, Australia.

Every athlete understands the importance of small victories, like personal records during a training session. These moments are crucial, for each personal record, every improvement, is a step closer to the ultimate goal. And the same applies to daily life. Turn your 'Done' list into a source of motivation. Pause to appreciate each success, every bit of progress, no matter how small. This reflection acts as a catalyst for further growth. It not only makes you aware of your progress, but also increases the joy in your pursuits. The result? Steady progress towards your personal goals, with more satisfaction and enjoyment along the way.

51

DO THE TONY HAWK

Tony Hawk in action during Xtreme Life Fest 2014, in Buenos Aires, Argentina.

Even when skateboarder and legend Tony Hawk was upside down, he saw the world right side up. His secret? He knew that every flip was an opportunity to see things from a new perspective. So, if your life feels like a half-pipe full of challenges, remind yourself: it's all a matter of perspective. Skate, laugh, and flip your view on things - do a Tony Hawk. Sometimes, you need a 360 to get everything back on track. ■

52

PUSH
YOUR
LIMITS

Freediver Alessia Zecchini in the breathtaking documentary The Deepest Breath.

Practicing extreme sports can have a therapeutic effect. There are several explanations for why it works. Doing something thrilling provides a sense of control, unlike many other aspects of life. Often, you can do much more than you think; and you learn that after feelings of fear and suffering, you can experience positive feelings. For instance, I tested myself by going snow-kiting in Norway. But you don't necessarily have to jump off a mountain in a wingsuit, and fly through a ravine, to push your limits. You can also push your boundaries at home. Put a drinking straw in your mouth and hold your nose, now breathe through the straw for 60 seconds. Set aside your timidity, an ode to risk. ■

53

ESPORTS IS IN THE DETAILS

Gamers during a gaming event in Bern, Switzerland.

In the digital arena, where the battle is just as fierce as on the field, the details make the difference between winning and losing. Take the PSV Esports team, which I had the honor of coaching for the KPN eDivisie Finals of 2024. Here, every millisecond of reaction time counts, every strategic move matters. Esports requires skills, strategic insight, mental alertness, physical fitness, and an unbreakable team spirit. Daily, they work on perfecting each of these components. Their success in the virtual arena proves that reaching the top is a matter of dedication to the smallest details. The greatest victories are hidden in the minutiae. ∎

54

RECOGNIZE YOUR BODY

Skater Jutta Leerdam after her 1,000-meter at the World Cup 2022 in Calgary, Canada.

Top speed skater Jutta Leerdam emphasizes that the menstrual cycle for women is not only a burden but a source of strength. In several interviews, she shares how she has learned to understand and use her cycle as a tool for better performance. She discovered that there are phases in her cycle when she feels stronger and more focused. Like Jutta, you can learn to recognize and utilize the unique rhythms of your body. Observe your energy levels, emotional states, and physical performance throughout the month. This way, you can align your activities and goals with the phases when you feel most powerful. ■

55

THE TRIPOD STOOL METHOD

A human tower of three young acrobats in Chinatown, Bangkok, Thailand.

Think of your goals as a three-legged stool. Each leg represents a different type of goal: outcome, performance, and process. Without one of these legs, your pursuit of success loses its balance.

Leg 1: You want to become a champion, the top scorer of your club, achieve something unique, or push a boundary. These are called outcome goals, serving as both the engine and source of inspiration.

Leg 2: What is the minimum time, distance, height, or score you need to achieve next month or next week? These are performance goals.

Leg 3: Process goals. What small steps do you need to take every day so you don't lose sight of the ultimate goal, but actually bring about change? ■

56

MUSIC IS YOUR BODYGUARD

Juergen Gerlinger (left) plays a cello concert in an empty swimming pool in Ammerbuch-Entringen, Germany.

Depending on your needs, the situation, and even a specific task, music can help improve performance. It's the ideal upper or downer, useful for athletes in preparation for a competition. Personally, I use the track Blue in Green by Miles Davis to relax, focusing my attention on his trumpet playing. I often play this song during workshops, noticing that participants calm down after the first minute-and-a-half and pay better attention for the remainder of the session. When I want to peak, I frequently tune into radio stations FIP Groove or Eclectic 24 by KCRW. Or just because I want to dance with my kids for a bit. ■

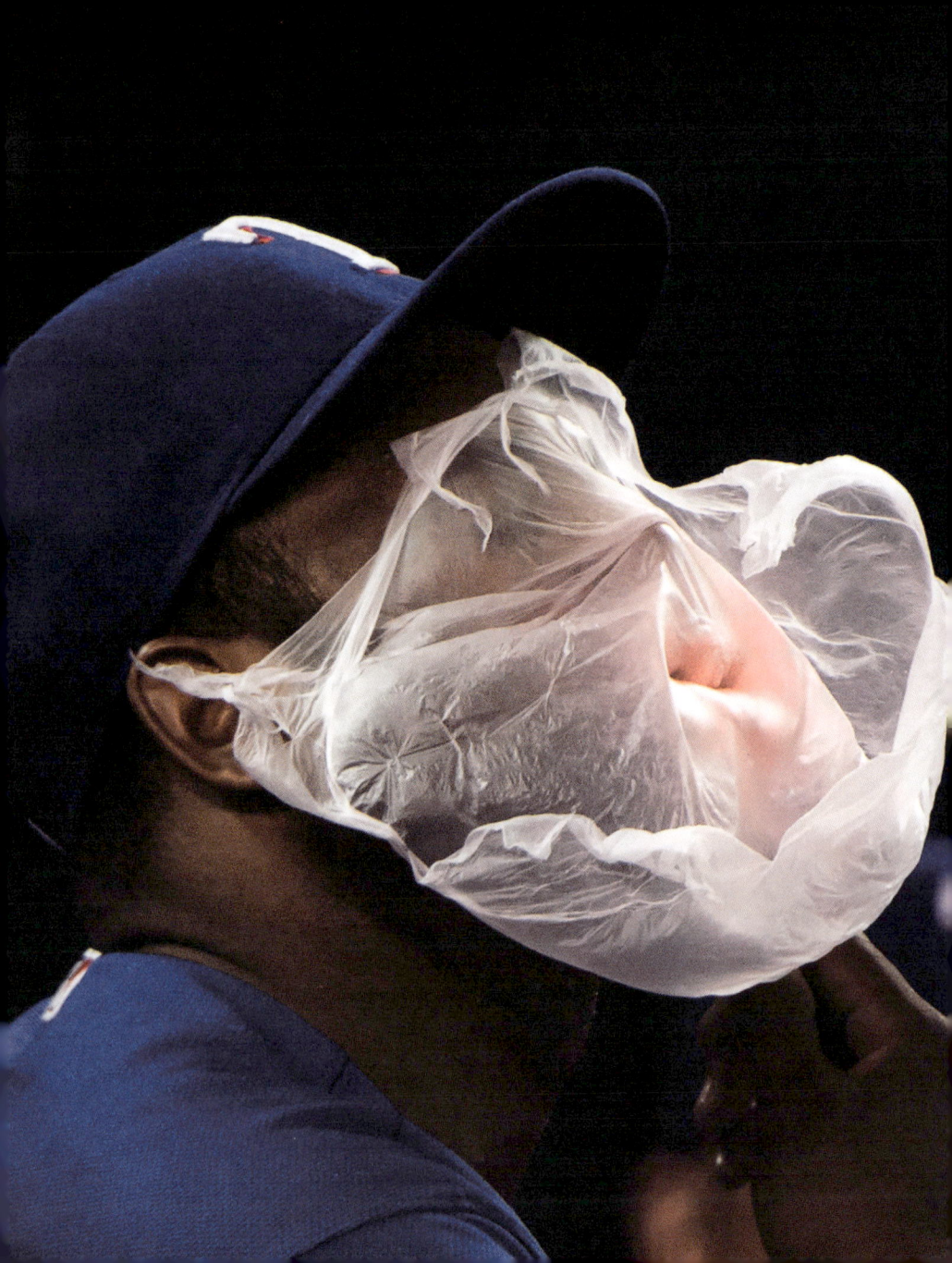

57

ATHLETES ARE JUST PEOPLE

Baseball player Hanser Alberto of Texas Rangers blows a bubble with bubble gum in Toronto, USA.

One in five elite athletes experience mental health issues. Athletes are increasingly open about this in the media, such as speed skater Stefan Groothuis, tennis player Naomi Osaka, or soccer player Gregory van der Wiel. Their advice for those experiencing issues: speak early with an expert, coach, clubmate, general practitioner, sports physician, or sports psychologist. An exploratory conversation can make a world of difference. At the TeamNL centers, we offer a consultation hour where athletes and coaches can drop by easily. Let's continue to break the stigma together. ■

THE ALI

YE

58

IT WILL BE A KILL AND A THRILLA AND A CHILLA WHEN I GET THE GORILLA IN MANILLA

Muhammad Ali spoke these words leading up to his title fight against Joe Frazier on October 1, 1975. The statement meets the dictionary definition of a yell: a shouted, often rhyming slogan, usually in the context of a competition. Yelling can be strategic, to unsettle the opponent or to pump yourself up. It is important to know that the beneficial - or detrimental - effect of yelling has a lot to do with the receiver's reaction to the shout. As an athlete, it is your job not to allow yourself to be psychologically influenced by the other's yell, says prototype yeller and tennis player John McEnroe. In short, drive the other person crazy, and don't let yourself be driven crazy. ∎

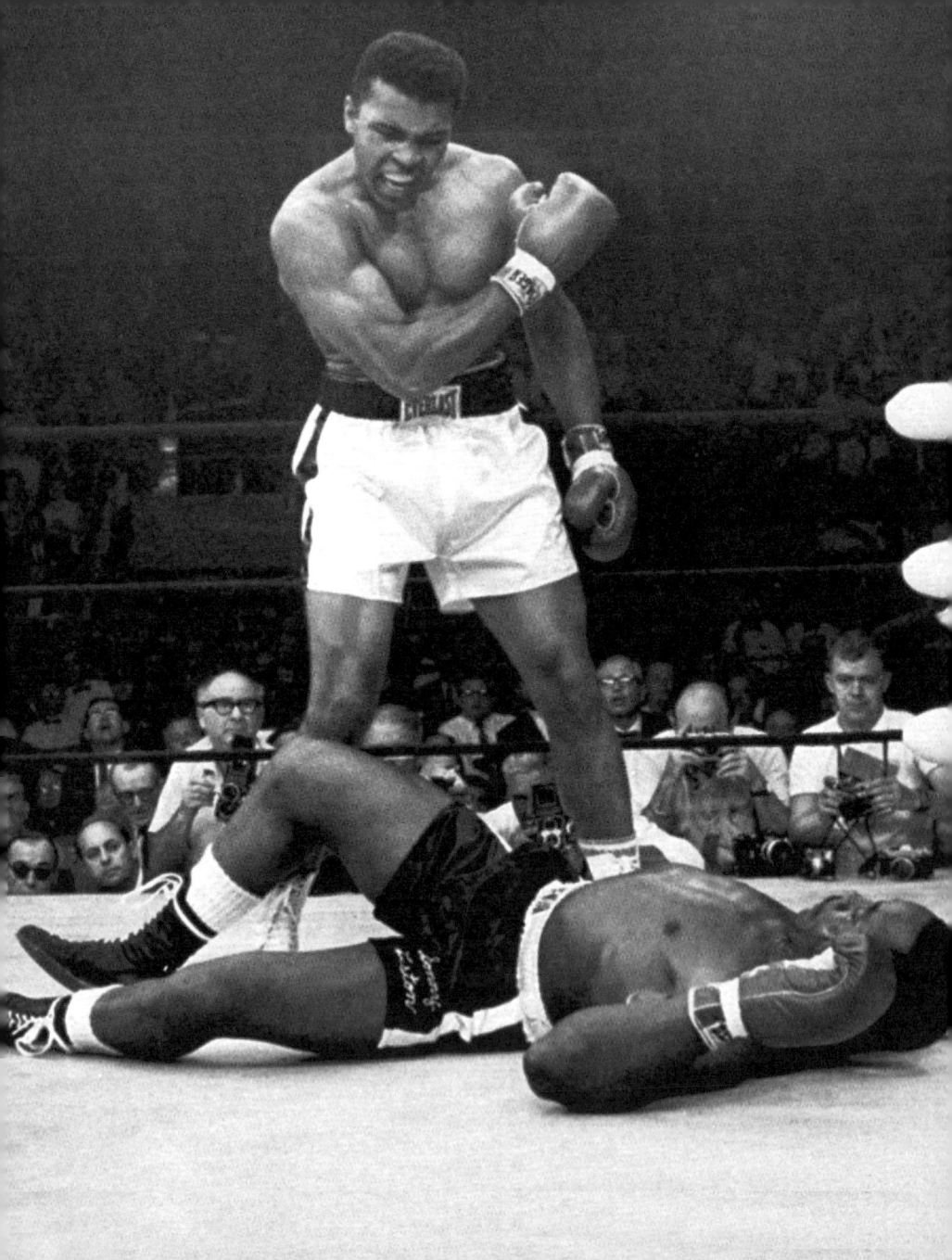

59

THE TWO TURBOS OF SELF-TALK

Muhammad Ali in action after his first-round knockout against Sonny Liston in St. Dominic's Arena, Lewiston, USA, 1965.

There are two turbos under the hood of self-talk: the motivator and the instructor. The motivator is your inner cheerleader, ready to pull you through a tough moment with a powerful: "You got this!" The instructor is your tactical and technical guide, leading you before and during your performance with focused advice like: "Keep your focus!" Speed king Usain Bolt showed how this works for him when he sprinted to gold with a simple yet effective, "Yo, this is good!" after the first few meters. Self-talk can be a personal powerhouse, whether you're accelerating or fine-tuning. •

60

CHOOSING
IS
FOR
WIMPS

Recovery after a triathlon in Almere, the Netherlands (3.8 km swimming, 180 km cycling, followed by a 42.2 km marathon).

The triathlon isn't just about sports - it's an ode to the limitless human spirit. Born from a bet to determine the most versatile athlete, it combines swimming, biking, and running into one epic challenge. It's the perfect storm of endurance, strategy, and sheer joy. And it shows you that you're capable of much more than you think. Stop choosing - pull on that wetsuit, pedal hard, and run towards victory. Because in the world of triathlon, more is always better! ■

61

PRO-CRASTINATOR? DON'T BE A DRAMATIZER!

After a flood of the Geul, a river in Valkenburg, the Netherlands, two young people smoke a cigarette.

Procrastination is the art of waiting for a better version of yourself. Sound familiar? Procrastination is human; everyone does it at times. But think of a top athlete. Imagine if Usain Bolt had decided to postpone his training because he'd have 'more energy tomorrow.' Would he ever have become the fastest man in the world? Probably not. The secret to his success? Starting. Even when you don't feel like it. What are you postponing? Take out that list. Look at the smallest step you can take right now, make that step even smaller, and begin. Even if it's just for 5 minutes. Overcoming procrastination doesn't mean waiting for perfect conditions, but starting despite imperfection. ■

62

TAKE
A WALK

At an intersection in Munich, Germany, 32 traffic signs refer to crossingwalks.

An hour's walk is the best and at the same time the cheapest advice I can give you as a sports psychologist. It's simple and amazingly effective; it decelerates life and boosts your creativity. Walking three times a week for 40 minutes keeps the part of the brain responsible for planning and memory healthy.

What's more, walking for thirty minutes a day can reduce symptoms of depression by 36 percent and drastically lower the risk of heart disease. Tip: download the 'Ommetje' app from the Dutch Brain Foundation. This app makes walking even more fun. You can walk together with friends, family, or colleagues without being in the same place. After every walk, you also get an interesting brain fact. ■

63

STICK
TO
THE
PLAN

Canoeist Sbonelo Khwela during a training session in KwaZulu-Natal, South Africa.

Skating coach Gerard Kemkers always used his fingers to signal during competitions, until he opted for a whiteboard during a crucial 10,000-meter speed-skating event at the 2010 Winter Olympics. It was a decision with far-reaching consequences. His pupil, Sven Kramer, ended up in the wrong lane due to an incorrect instruction, resulting in disqualification. Kemkers saw it as the biggest blunder of his career. Stick to your plan, especially when the pressure mounts. ■

#64

LOST
IN
TRANSLATION

Croatian model Ivana Knoll as a supporter during the 2022 World Cup football quarter-final at the Doha Stadium, Qatar.

Sport unites, but cultures interpret gestures and expressions in their own ways. A high-five, hug, or even a silent nod can provoke surprisingly different reactions around the world. At international tournaments, cultural misunderstandings sometimes lead to unintentionally comical moments, such as when a hug is considered a gesture of victory in one culture and too intimate in another. For example, in Russia, a laugh is truly reserved for close friends. Learn the local language of celebration. ■

65

THE POWER OF GENTLENESS

Japanese Jigorō Kanō, the founder of judo.

Judo is the art of balance, self-control, and respect. The 'gentle way' teaches us that true strength lies in flexibility and cleverly utilizing your opponent's power. Judo's founder, Jigorō Kanō, introduced principles such as Seiryoku Zenyo (maximum efficiency with minimum effort) and Jita Kyoei (mutual welfare and benefit). By also applying these principles off the mat, you learn to claim your space confidently and firmly, while respecting your own limits and those of others. Judo teaches us that victories are not achieved by overpowering the other, but through inner growth and overcoming your own weaknesses with grace and respect. ∎

66

BORIS BECKER'S TONGUE

Tennis player Boris Becker takes a risk with his serve, 1988.

Your body language reveals not just your physical condition but also what's going on in your mind. During an Oktoberfest in Munich, Andre Agassi explained to his rival Boris Becker why he had often won against 'Boom! Boom!' Becker: Agassi had noticed that Becker always stuck out his tongue in the direction of his serve. He kept an eye on Becker's mouth for five years and ultimately won 10 of their 14 matches. Pay attention to body language: your rival sees more than you think. ■

67

MAKE THE LEAP

Novice Ryan Claus practising for his first jump from the 10-meter tower.

Don't be paralyzed by fear; it's merely a natural response that you can overcome with courage and persistence. Take diver Guurtje Praasterink. Despite her fear, she regularly jumps from a 10-meter-high diving tower, even during World Championships. By doing this, she not only rose above her fear but also managed to qualify for the Olympic Games.

Whether you are facing a presentation at work or a personal challenge, feel the fear and do it anyway. Start with small steps outside your comfort zone and systematically build up to larger goals. Take a deep breath, focus, and make the leap. ■

68

OVERCOME YOUR LIFE'S RULES

Ntando Mahlangu competes in the long jump event at the Olympic Stadium during the 2020 Paralympic Games in Tokyo, Japan.

I must …
I have the idea that I must …
I notice that I have the thought that I must …

Place one of your own rules of life after no. 1. For example: I must have two legs to be able to do the long jump.

In no. 2, that becomes: I have the idea that I have to have two legs to be able to do the long jump. Do you notice that you already have greater leeway with no. 2?

And in no. 3, that you are having your life lived for you a little less by your own rule of life?

Absorb what happens. This exercise ensures that you experience your rules of life with their associated feelings and thoughts less rigidly. You feel more room and flexibility. Wanna bet? ■

69

NOT CHOOSING IS ALSO A CHOICE

Kayaker Vilayat Hussain trains on a self-built rowing machine in Kashmir, India.

Dilemmas: we face them every day. Athletes, just like you, constantly debate: to continue or to quit, to change coaches or not? But every hesitation, every delay is also a choice. Or, as psychologist Russ Harris says, realizing that you are always choosing, even by not choosing, gives you back control. Start your day with the mantra: "Today, I will base my choices on what really matters." Just like an athlete who carefully selects their equipment, knowing that innovation can make the difference between winning and losing. Your choices in life are like selecting the right equipment: every decision counts. ■

70

TRAIN YOUR FOCUS MUSCLE

Photographer Greg Armfield at work in Nairobi National Park, Kenya.

Multitasking makes us dumb. Each time we shift our focus to something else, it costs us concentration. In a world full of notifications, social media, and ads, your ability to concentrate really is your secret weapon. And athletes know: concentration can be trained. Find out why your focus sometimes falters - maybe due to too many or too few stimuli, or a lack of energy. The OHIO principle (Only Handle It Once) is a golden rule. Touching something? Finish it. That's how. I wrote this book in several years. My strategy? Cluster your tasks, listen to your favorite music, take regular breaks, use a 'do not disturb' signal, schedule theme days, and keep your phone out of sight. Focus Like a Pro! ■

71

CLOSE YOUR EYES TO GOLD

Zuid-Koreaanse boogschutter Dong-Hyun richt op intuïtie naar goud.

At the 2012 Olympics, South Korean archer Im Dong-Hyun shocked the world by breaking two world records despite having a visual acuity of 20/200 (which is technically considered blind). Rather than being limited by his sight, he focused on his technique and the sensations of the shot. This approach and training beyond visual limitations serve as a powerful example for many. Practice being in the moment, and focus your attention on the task at hand. This is how you find success, regardless of limitations. ∎

72

CHOOSE YOUR DONOR SPORT

Poland's Iga Swiatek after winning her tennis final in 2022, San Diego, USA.

Taekwondo training helps to improve kicking, striking, turning, balancing, and falling skills. The contribution one sport can make to another is demonstrated by Wormhoudt, Teunissen, and Savelsbergh's renowned Athletic Skills Model. A prime example is soccer player Ibrahimovic. Just look at his back heel kicks and stunning bicycle kicks. The wonder goal is his trademark, partly thanks to taekwondo. But there are more surprising combinations that can make a difference: think of a soccer goalkeeper playing badminton to enhance his reaction time and footwork; a speed skater who kitesurfs to train glide balance; or Michael Jordan who took up baseball to get better at throwing, catching, and aiming. What's your donor sport? ■

73

WHAT WOULD MY IDOL DO?

A Trump fan meets Donald Trump in Las Vegas, USA.

When in doubt, ask yourself: "What would my idol do?" This simple yet powerful question can give you direction. It's like a mental compass, guided by the values and principles of someone you admire. This approach not only transforms how you make decisions but also how you grow as a person. Play the hero card, and find your way in both sports and life. ∎

74

POWER DOWN

Head coach Simon Goodwin during a Melbourne Demons training session in Australia.

Without rest, there are no peak performances. Recovery is every coach's secret weapon. Pressure and stress are like shadows that follow you everywhere, but the light is found in moments of rest. The success of top scorers lies not just in their training, but in their ability to recover. And that applies to you too, coach. Take time to switch off. Become aware of your physical and mental state. Listen to your body and mind. Feeling the pressure mount? Step out of the arena for a bit. Seek diversion, share moments with loved ones, or finding pleasure in a hobby. Recovery is not accidental; it requires planning. A 'power down' strategy is your ticket to lasting success. Have you scheduled your recovery yet? ∎

75

FINISH IT!

Dutch skating championships (1976) in Groningen; Jos Valentijn starts off well here.

Speed skater Jos Valentijn was on his way to claim the 1976 World Allround Championships, but fate struck a blow during the final race. Two false starts cost him not just the title, but taught him a life lesson. Certainty is an illusion, even when the finish line seems within reach. No matter the size of your lead or your confidence in victory, it is crucial to stay focused. It's only over when it's truly over. ∎

CREDITS

#39 Helmut Fohringer | EPA | ANP
#40 Frater Schreykamp
#41 Ian Walton | Getty Images
#42 Mustafa Kurt | Anadolu Agency | Getty Images
#43 John Walton | Alamy | ANP
#44 Twitter
#45 Stephane de Sakutin | AFP | ANP
#46 E-Bay | foxyprinting.co.uk
#47 Jason Getz | USA TODAY Sports | Getty Images
#48 Mark Thompson | Red Bull Content Pool
#49 Dick Huber
#50 Matt Turner | EPA | ANP
#51 Gabriel Rossi | Latin Content | Getty Images
#52 Thanks to Netflix
#53 Peter Schneider | EPA | ANP
#54 Erik Pasman | ProShots
#55 Jack Taylor | AFP | ANP
#56 Christoph Schmidt | DPA | ANP
#57 Nathan Denette | The Canadian Press | AP | ANP
#58 Frater Schreykamp
#59 John Rooney | AP | ANP
#60 Klaas Jan van der Weij | klaasjan.photography
#61 Marcel van den Bergh | @marcel_van_den_bergh
#62 Lukas Barth-Tuttas | EPA | ANP
#63 Kevin Sawyer | Bull Content Pool
#64 Friedemann Vogel | EPA | ANP
#65 Jigoro Kano
#66 Moenkebild | Ullstein bild | Getty Images
#67 Paul Tolenaar | paultolenaar.com
#68 International Olympic Committee (IOC) Thomas Lovelock | AFP
#69 Dar Yasin | AP | ANP
#70 Jonathan Caramanus | Green Renaissance | wwf.org.uk
#71 Richard Drew | AP | ANP
#72 Gregory Bull | AP | ANP
#73 Ruth Fremson | The New York Times | ANP
#74 Michael Dodge | Getty Images
#75 Bert Verhoeff | Nationaal Archief | Anefo

THANK YOU TO:

Aernoud - for the sharpness and encouragement when I needed it.

Peter - for the brilliant creative process.

Frank - for the images that surprise and challenge.

Joris - for your magic with texts.

Floris - for setting up the 'extra' help.

Rodney - for help with the translation.

Fellow (sports) psychologists from TeamNL and VSPN - for the inspiration, collaborations, and brainstorming about our beautiful profession.

Eefje - for the opportunities I've received at TeamNL.

Nienke - for the opportunities I've received at BrabantSport.

Colleagues from BrabantSport - for the collaboration that is far from over.

Marieke - for your cool idea to launch the book.

Jules and other colleagues - for the pleasant conversations, even when things were tough.

Many athletes, coaches, and teams - for your lessons, and the new ones that will follow.

My in-laws - for the Saoto soup, 'Pom', and games of 'Troefcall'.

NL - for the beautiful places to write and be outdoors.

My parents, 'Paake' and 'Momo' - for your unconditional love, even when I again come up with crazy plans.

Anne - for your optimism.

Wanita - for your love and indispensable support, 'broodje kaas'!